In Infinite Possibilities… We Must Be Happy Somewhere

Kelly Mowers

Presentation by *BookLeaf Publishing*

Web: www.bookleafpub.com

E-mail: info@bookleafpub.com

ISBN: 9789363312678

First edition 2024

For D.

CONTENTS

New Moon

Who are you?

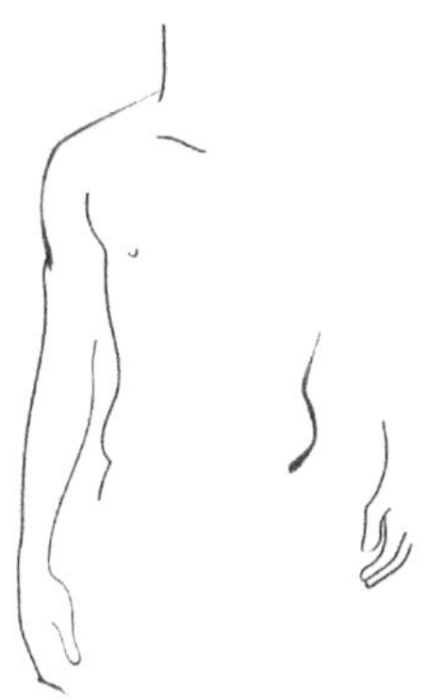

Who are you?
This warm skin stuck to mine
Closer to my heart than my own breath
Memories
Flooding
Visions flashing of you as
A past life torrid lover
Tracing constellations on my skin
Explaining the light years needed to travel
To be here
An alien bringing
Starlight wisdom in your
Touch
Revealing my body like a prophecy
That you have always known
As I sensed you for years

In the moment before waking
Just out of reach
Your taste and your scent
Slowly fading
You are no longer the mist
You have taken form with
The vision from a dream
Who walks through the door,
Whole and yet
Impermanent
Anicca
I pull you closer
As time laughs,
Nodding towards morning
I listen to you breathe
I watch your face in the
Threatening dawn,
Study every legend
Written in the lines of
Your eyes,
Knowing that there will never be
Enough moments
To know all of you
Your secrets
Brought across time
Connect us
I move the damp curl from your cheek
And brush my lips over yours
I touch you

Feel your body reaching out
Breathe in your air
Like a diver gasping at the surface
As if my next intake
Will be my glorious last
Even Poseidon is envious
As he strikes down his trident
Head bent back
Sending waves across higher dimensions.
Resting on your rising chest,
Staring out
Wondering if
In parallel universes,
Where our lives do not collide
Do I still wander?
Do I walk the night and curse the stars…
Wrapped only in that woven Navajo blanket?
On the edge of the cliff, where
I first heard you
Over the waves
Calling from galaxies far, far away
Yet, we lay together
In this tiny universe
Two fallen strangers
Creating a poem
While my parallel lives
Stare in envy
At our brazen touch
And abandoned fears

And I say goodbye to the roaming shadow
I leave it with the howling dust
As it twists around the room
And scatters the papers
I so carefully stacked
And casts sand on the clothes
Strewn across the floor.
(Silmë Saila)

Orion

I trace Orion on your arm
You point to the sky
The Seven Sisters of Pleiades flee
Hiding in Taurus from
The hunter,
With his hounds
Even chaste Artemis
Couldn't resist
His shiny belt
Alnilam, Alnitak, Mintaka
Aligning with
The three Great Pyramids
Creating a pathway
From here to the heavens
While
Scorpio waits across the sky
For another chance
To pounce
We watch
Shooting stars

Sending wishes
To star systems
That may or may not still exist
I can't keep the worlds apart
They merge
And separate into
The Gates of Argonath,
The Pillars of the Kings
As two different bookends
Blurring the words in between
Sand in your teeth
My mouth reaches for yours
Your hands explore
My tongue kisses symbols
On your neck with
Shield knots,
Your chest with
The Vegvisir
Down past your stomach with
The Man in the Maze
Circling back up
Smelling your hair
The mist and swirls of sand and sea
The weight of your body
An anchor
From falling across the sky as
I whisper in your ear…
"Come with me."
Travelling again while I am awake

To an old man chanting in the desert
Asking why I always run so far
He draws a circle in the sand
His one hand points up
The other down
I look into him
But can’t grasp
His words
He smiles and looks up,
“These are your stars.”

If We Could Start Over

In a multiverse of endless possibilities…
I would keep searching
For the timeline
Where I know what I know
But
…We haven't met yet

Bank Street Beach

I dressed for this meeting,
But
I left my hair full of sand
My wrap from last night in
My briefcase beside me
As if keeping these remnants of last night
Would keep your body and smell next to me
I watch my colleague write on his whiteboard
His exaggerated hand motions
Expounds his educational arguments
I am not following
Not because it is complex
Rather
Biting my bottom lip
My eyes travel
Back to my train ride
Paris bound
The rhythmic, hypnotic motion
That builds up slowly
As the train speeds along the tracks

How the vibrations travel up my seat
If you close your eyes,
You can really feel it
Hoping not to go over a bump
…or hoping no one notices if you do
Is stimulating
The way I press the book into my lap
Shifting in my seat
Looking out at all the possibilities
Breathing and smiling
At my secret
Laughing at all the blank faces
Staring straight ahead
Can no one else feel it?
This life
This bloody bottom lip
My eyes close
I spin in my computer chair
Dipping on a falling rollercoaster
Barely concentrating
My colleagues are rapidly rambling
Remembering your hands on my body
Feeling them move up my skirt
Makes this meeting
Agonising
The memory of your lips
A soft gasp
Escapes
People turn

Blushing I
Pull the papers to my chest
Apologising
Recalling something you said…
Astral projection, popping and
The tip of your nose
This new world
Drowning out the
Droning voices
Clicking pens
Eyes wide
I realise
Diving into your mind
Makes me want your skin
Teach me
Run your hands through my hair
I feel all of you under my fingers
That can barely type the
Ideas being thrown out
Craving your tongue
I try to follow
But my mind wanders
To the beach,
Bank Street Beach,
Swirling with sand and red wine,
The stars, the wind, the waves
And the rhythmic, hypnotic motion
Of your body pressing into mine.

In a multiverse of endless possibilities…
We'll meet on “Solsbury Hill”
“In My Life” and
Frolic in “Fields of Gold”
Forever

Henna Tattoos

A skunk
lies
on the side
of the road
tasting
metallic
soft fur
blowing
contrasting the
frozen corpse
left there
decaying.
Parking
at night
facing
Orion
staring
at stars.
Twirling
in snow

catching
snowflakes
my tongue
kissing
your body.
Trying
not
to think
pushing
you
back down
like secrets
lost
in life.
Ripping off
your shirt
lying
beside you
talking
holding
your hand.
Fading to
lying naked
the candle
dancing
breathing
exploring.
My tongue
outlining

a draft
reaching
over for
the henna cone
marking
pale skin
drawing
a design
from naval
to neck.
Tattooing
dots
lines
swirls
cold ink
on hot skin
shivering
arms spread out
a willing sacrifice.
Closing eyes
feeling
every breath
every sigh
alchemic
alphabetic
arousal
arising
magickal sigils
you can't understand

covering
your skin.
Feeling me
taking you
reaching
remembering
the henna
is not dry,
you become
a moving statue
listening
breathing
gasping
watching
hips rising
falling into me.
Back arching
careful
not to
destroy the
intricate designs
whispering
all over your body
in the dark light.
Your eyes asking
me to explain
this universe
a map on
your skin of

swirling
streaking stars
spying
in the future
of secrets
never known
wondering
what I wish
I could tell you.
I smile
sighing sadly
knowing
you will
fade
away like
this henna map
existing
only in my mind.

Pyramids

I live on the south coast
Of Crete
Some days, I swear I can see Egypt
From my balcony
A wavering palace
A mirage of a
Glorious mythological world
In reality, the
Red dust that
Blows to Crete
Covering everything and
Filling our lungs is the
Closest I have been to Egypt
In this life
But I have lived there before
It calls to me
Just as Greece had
Whispered
Come home

Come back
Knossos was my home
I wept when I visited the ruins
I was La Parisienne,
The Minoan Lady
Lost in the labyrinth
Painted on a wall
I found my Minoan soulmate
But he doesn't remember this life
And just as the
Santorini volcano erupted
Sending lava shooting
Across the sea
Burning us all alive and
Destroying our civilization
His bonfire of rage
Consumed us again
And our skin burned
Until I left

In the quiet of starting over
I hear a new whisper
Come home
Come back
Giza calls
So, travelling to meet you,
My first love
From years ago
There, of all places,

Made waiting
So hard
Years apart
And lives lived
Without contact
Creates a sexual
Society of secrets
Imagining
Pharaohs and Priestesses
Gold and turquoise
Indiana Jones
And alien beings
Camels and deserts
Mysteries and madness
Gods and Goddesses
Worshipping your naked
Statue as we overlook
One of the Wonders of the
Ancient World

There are no words for it
When you are here
Staring at the Pyramids
From your balcony
We brunch at the Lounge
We walk in the desert
I keep screaming,
"We are in the
Freaking desert!"

"Stop speaking Greek,"
You laugh
We find the photographic
Angle to get all the
Pyramids
In one shot
I make sand angels
While baking in the sun
We buy tickets to go into
A Pyramid the next day
We are melting clocks as
We make our way back
I think I will never breathe again
I will never find enough water
I refuse to ride a camel
I sense the owners
Are cruel to them
And we make it back
To the air conditioning
I pass out on the bed
You take a shower
I awaken to you pulling off my pants
And carrying me to the bath
Rose petals float and
You rub a sea sponge
On my forehead
Dripping it on my breasts
Massaging my back
And I am revived

You join me
And we don't leave
The room again that day

That night lights dance
A kaleidoscope of colours
Across the Pyramids
And glow up into the heavens
The stars answer back
You tell me,
The three stars
Of Orion's belt
Alnitak, Alnilam, and Mintaka
Align with the Pyramids
I see it now
Naked on the balcony
My hands tied to the
Metal bar above me
You tease me
With a feather,
You stole from the
Flower arrangement
In the lobby
And your tongue
Circles my breasts
As it slowly works its way down
You slide to your knees
Staring up at me
My head tilts back

Breathing deeper
Staring at the Pyramids
Imagining
I am Isis
My light shines up to
Orion's belt
Connecting us
To the stars above

A cigarette glowing orange
On the balcony near us
Someone is watching
Someone is listening
To us
In the dark
I make out a shadow
Of a man
I can feel
Our eyes lock
And he doesn't move
For a country where I spend my days
Covered from shoulder to knee
This enthrals me
I love you, Isis
I love you, Hathor
I see my goddesses
I see me
Here
I am similar to now

But my hair was black
And I wore strange make-up
I think maybe we can make it
This time
Maybe we can start again

We are worshipping each other
Floating in stardust
I hear the
Voyeur release
The orange glow falls
From his mouth
I smile in the dark
I am worshipped
I am a queen
I am connected to everything
…I am home
…I am free

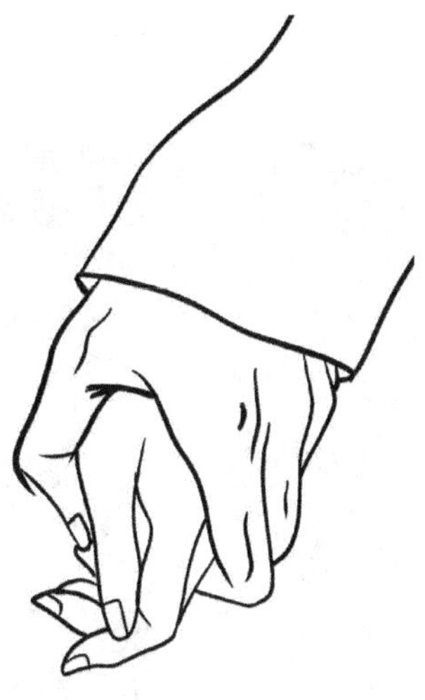

In a multiverse of endless possibilities…
We travel interdimensionally
We meet beings from universes
We never knew existed
We never grow tired of the way our
Hands feel being held by each other

Forest Fire

Infinite timelines
Creating comets of chaos
Regrets
Ceasing to exist
Bad decisions
Not even a contemplated thought
One kiss or a few thousand
Never happen
Wars cease
Food is in abundance
We are One
There is no sorrow
For the loss of someone
You never knew
But I wouldn't change
Meeting you

I can see those timelines
Where we never pass
On the same street or
Run in the same circles
I am happy with a perfectly
Nice… mate
Never knowing
How it feels to be touched
By you
To feel your lips
Under the night sky
Your tongue
Moving down my neck
Never knowing your
Thoughts and ideals
That sparked the dying
Remnants of a forgotten fire
Yes, I am perfectly happy
In my blissful ignorance
Of you.
I marry wearing white
In a church of brightly coloured windows
We live in an old Victorian
We eat dinner at 5:00
We go for Sunday drives
We have two children
One boy, one girl
And vacation on the Cape
We work our 8 hours

We watch TV before bed
In front of a gas faux fire
We have sex on the weekends
It's a perfectly delightful life
And then there are the
Timelines with you…
We plan big plans
We change the world
We meet all over the globe
We can't keep our clothes on
We read each other to sleep
We write poems that
Should be censured
Burning with a brightness
Causing blindness
With an otherworld
intensity
Caught in
Timeline connections from
previous lifetimes
On other dimensions
And we keep crossing paths
Our souls recognize each other
Our bodies simply respond
Our minds scream to run and
Our innocent hearts
Are the repeated victims
Slain in slow motion
Bleeding, bruised, and rotting

Like dead animals
Decaying
But I would still wish upon the
Falling stars from
Any Star Systems
That may or may not still exist
As you whisper in my ear
On a dark beach where
Orion winks
And the moon
Is nowhere to be seen
I choose you
The timelines of intensity
And pain with the
Momentary hope of
A love that is over
Before it begins
And I think this is the lesson
We need to learn
The reason we come back
Lifetime after lifetime
Because we need to think,
What is a life
Of mediocrity
When you have known
Lives and loves
That have travelled
Interdimensionally
To meet again and again

Over and over
Wherever you are
I am searching for you
At the supermarket
The pharmacy
At high school football games
In my dreams
In my books
I see you just before waking
I crave you
I taste you
I choose you
Even knowing we will
Burn like a forest fire
Fed by strong winds
Leaving nothing but
Charred wood and death
Our hearts smouldering
Inside the skeletal
Remains
Of two souls
Who love each other

In a multiverse of endless possibilities…
Mother Gaia is thriving
We are all One
Embracing under
The Tree of Life

Past Lives and Parallel Universes

Explain parallel universes
Spiralling through space and
Past life connections
Mysteries and magic
Astral travel and an array of auras
Crystals and seashells
Myths and legends
Stars and pyramids
Lost languages and light codes
…War and peace
Let me taste the sand
In your teeth
Let our hair tangle
In the wind
My hands on your pale skin
The moon staring down
As the stars streak

You speak
Softly,
Slowly,
Seductively…
I am the centre of the universe
You tell me to trust you
Assure me I can trust you
I knew
I knew better
I knew better and didn't care
I wanted you
Your wounds and pain
Your grief and sadness
Your heart full of swords
I wanted to heal you
Hold you
Reassure you
Love you
As if love was enough
To cure the dank darkness
In the depths of your despair
We make love
You read me to sleep
I don't care that you tell me
You always read to her
No one had ever read to me
Sleeping, smiling, stretching
I wake to reach for you
But your back is shaking

In the moonlight
You are crying
Huge sobs of silent
Gasps
And to this day
I wonder if I should have held you
While you thought of her
And the life you needed to leave behind
All that drama, chaos, and love
You wanted to stay
You wanted to stay, and she begged you
You wanted to stay, and she begged you to leave
I quietly turned the other way
Those tears were pure private pain
In a rental where you don't even have a bedroom
My tears drench your daughter's pillowcase
Flowing until you fall asleep
Two waterfalls and a
Vast space between us
I will never be Her
And I shouldn't wish to be
I wouldn't have minded
I wouldn't have minded pretending
I definitely wouldn't have minded pretending
For just a bit longer
I only want to love you
And I do
You see
You have no control over that

I see us in a parallel universe
So in love
Awakening
Travelling
Changing the world
And in our past lives
We knew each other
So steamy, but
Futile thoughts here
In this version of reality
I am merely a mention
In the chapter
Titled
"The Nightmare After Divorce"
I will not star
I will not star or even be
I will not star or even be a thought
In your new book
Of life
Trying to sneak out
Grabbing my clothes and purse
Every movement echoes
You stir
I kiss you goodbye
I don't look you in the eye
You seem so confused
Maybe awoken from some version
Where you were with Her
I go downstairs and realise I left my shoes

Throw them away
Throw every thought
Memory
Laugh
Glance
Seashell
Poem
Ridiculous gift and
Tubberware of hope
Throw them all
I let myself out
The door locks behind me
Gasping
Realising I was holding my breath
Bare Feet on gravel
Cannot stop me from running
To the car
Door slams
Birds stir
Bloody toes
Runny nose
Seatbelt on
Headlights
Reverse
Drive
Mascara flows
Empty roads
Windows down
Morning mist

An orange glow…
…Is it the hole in the muffler
Waking up the world
As I fly down the road or
The sobs, shrieks, and howls
Emanating from my soul?

In a multiverse of endless possibilities…
There is a timeline where
I am not sending wishes to
Star systems that
No longer exist

Kindling

The first time I met you
You said,
"I am literally the essence of what not to talk about at a party…
My life's purpose encompasses the taboo topics of peace, politics, and religion.
It's no wonder I am not invited out often."
We laughed…
But as you spoke about
All the things that matter
I felt my soul
Begin to
Flicker
Every word
Like a damp match
Struck over and over
Rocks repeatedly rubbing

Stones striking savagely
Twirling twigs of tinder
Creating a spark,
And
I was the dry kindling…
Everything you said
Lit me on fire

In a multiverse of endless possibilities…

Full Moon
Quests in High School Literature

Come closer…
Let me
Whisper
Thoughts through
Dreams and
Visions
You cannot understand
Like
The lost languages of
Past lifetimes where
The Wheel of Fortune
Turns and
Divine intervention
Laughs
Did you really think it wouldn't happen?

Standing
Watching a man
Silhouetted
Black against the moon
Looking
Out at the water
His Gatsbian hand reaching
Across
To the lands waiting for him to discover
The greenlight is truly Emerald,
While the stars and mist swirl,
White like a thousand
Lightning bugs in flight

Odysseus
Steps into the
Unknown
Beckoning with
Stories
Waiting to
Evolve
Remembering
Ithaca
Not looking back
Or
Only forward
A journey
Of now
Embracing time

Feeling this jasmine-scented moment
Tasting the sea bird's cry
Searching the stars
Charting
This night
Clutching the
Spinning clock
As the hands dig
Deep
Holding the
Knowing of
All the possibilities
I step back
To watch you pass

As you glide through the airport of endless windows
Imagine the Sun King
As a child
Playing in the Hall of Mirrors and Light
With less lace and ruffles
And more comfortable shoes
Circling prisms
Dancing
Trying to catch the sun
A waltz
With Freedom
Knowing
Just knowing that
Destiny calls

Sometimes, I think of you
I am not as patient as Penelope
Or as daft as Daisy
I wish you well
Happiness and health
Love and Light
The beauty of
Unconditional Love
Is sad and freeing
I would never be Her
You would always be searching
Getting lost on islands with
Goddesses for seven years
Creating false kingdoms to impress
Only to find that
You will always be from the West Egg.

Who would chase a love like that?
Never being enough
Always being tested
Divine Runner, run
My love will always be with you
Divine partners meet again and again
In this lifetime and the next
Twin Flames have no choice
Like Catherine and Heathcliff
Our souls are one
Connected through
Heaven and Hell

Come closer,
Lie down next to me
Let us follow King Louis' lead
Enjoy the nights of passion
And drink
And when we are spent…
Let me whisper in your ear…
Thoughts through
Dreams and
Visions
You cannot understand
Like
The lost languages of
Past lifetimes where
The Wheel of Fortune
Spins and spins
The unfortunate fates of
The neverending
Tragedies of
Endless tales
Of those who loved too much

In a multiverse of endless possibilities…
I still
Choose you

My Favorite City

My head rests on your chest
Your fingers play with my hair
As you read from a book
Your glasses on the tip of your nose
I draw constellations lightly
On your stomach
By connecting the freckles
You beg me to stop
You are trying not to laugh and
You put down the book
and say,
Name your favourite city…

I say,
That's easy…
New Orleans.

In all the world?

Yes, New Orleans.

Why?
It's smelly and dirty…

New Orleans?
My New Orleans
Is alive
With a vibration
That is on a frequency
Of a faraway home
It is like nowhere else
That we know
The music
The food
The laughter
The magic
The colourful houses
The heat
The neon lights
The languages
The deep drums
And forlorn horns
Marching at midnight
You, getting swept up
And taking me in
The alley
Off Bourbon street
And then, on the
Metal laced balcony
Under the full moon

For all to see
A vampire
That the more
You suck
The stronger
I become
My ghost
Still wanders
Into all the jazz clubs
And voodoo parlours
No one ages here
In the French Quarter
I remain a maiden
Stuck in a time warp
Only just kissed
You still circle me
Like the hawk
Assessing my naivete
My willingness
To astral project
Here and there
Over and over
I am surprised
You bother to
Put your pants back on
We are just spiralling spirits
Stuck in an
Incessant loop
Eating an endless

Cauldron of Jambalaya
In a city
Where anything happens
Forget Roswell
They are all here
Walking among us
The Tarot Card Reader
The Seer
Signal me secretly as a
Starseed
We speak telepathically
Portraying the portal
Through our art
And yet… I still
Flash my young breasts
As you walk by
In hopes that you
Might throw me
Some stupid
Seventy cents
Sparkly
Shiny beads…

In a multiverse of endless possibilities…
We change the world together
"What a Wonderful World" we create

Changing the World

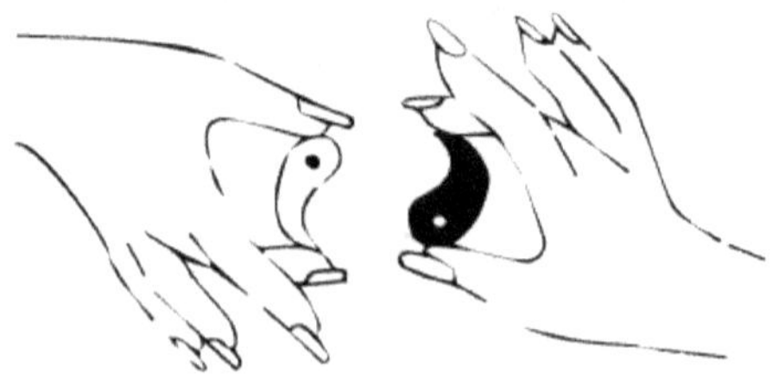

We separated to work on ourselves
On our missions
You are seeking peace
In religious conflicts
I am seeking peace
For refugees and women
Actually, we want oppression to end
Climate change to disappear
For all religions
To love each other
For Love to
Reign supreme
We are all love
We are all one
It should be simple enough
He is working in his world
And I am here,
Working in mine
We are going to help
Change the world

Separation is necessary
To grow
All Twin Flames
Burn alone
Until destiny
Until divine timing
Brings them back together
Nothing can destroy
The bond
If it is meant to be
You will find your way back to each other
But if you are false divines…
You will never connect again
But who wants what is not theirs anyway?
You came closer than any…

You are staying in one place for
Six months
I quickly send you several letters

Dearest D,
My mission is not menial
It is so big
I despair in where to begin
I think Alice Paul is turning in her grave
All she sacrificed so
Short skirts made of sequins shining on a dance floor

Doesn't equal a sacrificial offering of your body to the
Worshipping, slobbering, rough hands
Groping and riding you
As you enjoy the music.
Women need to carry signs
That glow in the blacklights
Hands off!
Like the red flags
The suffrages raised
Actually, pepper spray would be more effective
But that's illegal now
The work must continue
The calling does not stop
The Suffragettes starved in prison
Being forced fed
Beaten
Betrayed
Spit on
Rained on
Shamed
So that women today can vote…
So that women could simply have the right to vote in who ran their country
But that wasn't the only reason…
The American Suffragettes
Alice Paul,
Lucy Stone,
Ida B. Wells,

Elizabeth Cady Stanton,
Mary Church Terell,
Sojourner Truth,
and Susan B. Anthony
…to name a few in this country,
But this excludes the thousands of other women
Who join them in their
Fight for equality
For all humans
In all countries of this world
To be seen
As intelligent
As strong
As capable of ruling, running, reigning
As able to save sinking souls and serve as soldiers
As CEOs in the most prominent corporations
As Presidents, Prime Ministers, and Queens
As worthy of education…
As every other soul on this planet

Do you think the Suffragettes' work is done?
Do you think the spirits of the Suffragettes rest in peace knowing the fight is over?
Can we laugh and sigh in relief?
Roe vs. Wade is reversed
Will we lose the right to vote next?
Religion is back in public schools
But whose religion is it?

Close your eyes for a moment…
And think of the girls in Afghanistan, Iran,
Iraq…
Covered from head to toe
Beaten to death for showing their hair
Cowering behind a man while walking down a
street
Denied education
Denied freedom
Denied
Denied
Denied

Love,
Me

You write back!
I am in a refugee camp
With no internet
You are somewhere
You sent a news video
A month ago
Where you were
Sitting with two religious leaders
Who had wanted to kill each other
Somehow, you convinced them
To unite
You were all
Sitting at a table together

I couldn't understand the different languages
But it was so great to see you and
It was worth walking miles to
Find an internet connection
You sent me a letter
A handwritten letter
It is hard to believe it found me
And that this letter made it
Into my tent
"We Used to Wait" by Arcade Fire
Plays on repeat in my mind
You are excited
Things are moving in
The right direction
I can hear your smile
In your words
You tell me that I can't blame
Myself for being ordered
By authorities
To bring the woman and her child
Back to the camp
Where they were once again
Violently abused
But I had gone from finding them
A safe house
To driving them back to their
Abuser
Laws and rules are not always
Logical

If we had disappeared,
We all would have been arrested
Volunteers are being accused of
Smuggling refugees into
Europe
Of aiding people
Of trying to save people
You say that your work is also
Fragile
You never know when
Fighting will break out
I worry for your safety,
But we need to try to make
Things better
Right?

You ended your letter with
These thoughts,

My Dear,
Don't forget…
Do you remember the terror of
The US exit from Afghanistan?
A screaming sea of panic
Babies being handed to soldiers
Mothers, knowing that their baby would
Be better off with strangers than with the
Taliban
Secrets and Shadows

Surrounding this
Surrender to suffering

Where are our Suffragettes?
It is 2024
And the army of women
Is quiet…
Where is the outrage?
Where is the justice for our sisters?
Why do we turn away from
Girls being mutilated for being a girl
Why do we turn away from
Girls being shoved in a hut for days when menstruating
Why do we turn away from
Girls who are eight years old being married to 40-year-old men
Why do we turn away from
Girls and boys being sold into sex labour
Epstein's island is just one example of this travesty
One example
Of the Fallen Angels

We still have work to do
So, so, so much work to do
Yet we waver in the luxury of our comfort
In a world where we worry whether
We are beautiful enough

Smart enough
Rich enough
Equal enough
Enough is
Enough…
Think
Equality, equity, empathy
Earth
Do you feel me?

Love,
D

I write back to you,
But I doubt you
Will receive it
You are moving around
But will check your mail
In a certain city
One day
If you get there
It seems to me this will be
A letter that travels
Continuously
Around the world
But never finds
Its destination

I write,

Dearest D,
I feel you every night
You awaken
Just as I fall asleep
I love that moment
That touch
But I know this is not what you mean
I feel you
Look around…
Refugees are fleeing for their lives
Walking miles upon miles
With the hope of a better life
A promise
A dream
An idea of a better world
Other refugees
Selling everything they own
To put their families in rubber boats
To reach a Europe
That will be denied to so many
Push Backs of boats carrying women and children
To drown while no one claims them
Refugee camps
Eventually, setting them all "free."
With no money, language, or homes
Mothers, children, Grandmothers
Drowning in the Mediterranean Sea

Or wandering foreign cities,
Dirty, starving
With nothing but their dreams.
They are leaving everything they know
In hopes of staying alive
In a world where you are murdered for
Your religion
Your sex
Your cast
Your survival is full of suffering

We need to seize the spirit of the Suffragettes
We need to fight for those who cannot fight for
themselves.
We need to raise the red flags
For all women
For all children
For all… men
For all souls
That are oppressed,
Mutilated, humiliated, hunted

See how far we have come and
Congratulate ourselves
On these achievements
But we must also see
How far we have yet to go
Our fight is not over
Not until every woman, man, and child has

Food and shelter
The bare necessities to survive
Not until every girl and every child has the right
To education
The right to knowledge
Not until we are safe in our beliefs and not killed
Because of them
No more wars in the name of any Divine being
Not until the Earth is saved, our water clean, and
Our food abundant
So that all people of this planet have
Nourishment
Not until we see that we are all connected
One
The prophecy of Crazy Horse says,

"A world filled with broken promises, selfishness, and separations. A world longing for light again. I see a time of seven generations when all the colours of mankind will gather under the sacred Tree of Life, and the whole Earth will become one circle again…In that day, there will be those among the Lakota who will carry knowledge and understanding of unity among all living things, and the young white ones will come to those of my people and ask for wisdom…I salute the light within your eyes where the whole universe dwells. For when you are at that centre within you, and I am in that place within me, we shall be as one."

Only then will the world stop weeping
Only then will the universe unite
Only then will our religions embrace
Only then will the wars stop
Only then can people stop fleeing from their homes
Only then can our Sisters of old,
Our Goddesses,
Our Warrior Women,
Our Divine Feminines and
Our Suffragettes
Smile under the Great Tree and
Rest in peace

Love,
Me

Dearest D,
I hope you received my last letter.
I have not heard from you in months
No letters
No messages
No Whatsapp
It shows that you haven't been active
In months
There was unrest in your area

Killings started again
But surely you are okay
Just busy
With your life's work or
No internet anywhere
I have had to hide
My phone from myself
To stop checking it
I almost tackled
The man bringing letters
Silence is so
Stifling,
Heavy, and
Final…

I don't think I will send this letter
I don't believe you
Would be able to read
The smeared ink
Anyway
I miss you
Please be safe

Love,
Me

In a multiverse of endless possibilities…
We end war and starvation
The world is abundant and in peace
And then we stay home
In our bed
Looking out at the ocean
From a wall of windows
…And we spend a lot of time in bed

Paris

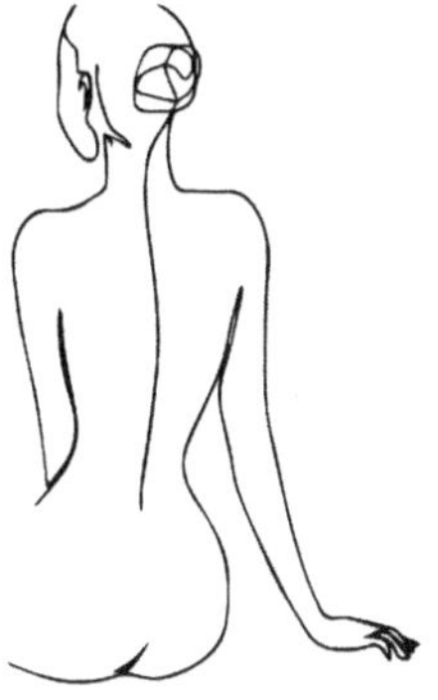

It seemed a good idea
To meet in Paris…
Me, travelling up from Bilbao
The screams and rhythm of the tracks
Slowly building momentum
Almost a full day
I thought I would never get there…
You, flying in from Ireland
Who doesn't want to meet in Paris?
And we embrace at the airport
Like they do in the movies
Lovers that were torn apart
By war, misfortune, misunderstanding
Immediately, like a reflex
My hands move to undress you
But trying to act sophisticated
Like the women with dark glasses,
Perfect red lipstick, and

Silk scarves wrapped around their hair
I pull myself back
Oui, oui…we are in Paris
Mon Amoureux, the Eiffel Tower awaits
Mon Chérie…
We smile as we wait for your luggage
That smile of a shared secret
Barely keeping our clothes on
In the Uber
Until we finally arrive at our
Home for the week
Croissants and coffee are waiting
With pamphlets for every museum
But we don't notice these for hours
We explore the city
But even the Louvre
Becomes a lesson in
Appreciating art
While wanting to tear your clothes off
Mona Lisa's smile understands
We picnic in the
Gardens,
Drinking champagne
Talking of futures together
We visit Dali, Monet, Rodin, Claudel
We even venture to Versailles
He buys a statue of
The Thinker

Which I now know is the perfect present to
himself
I buy him the Sun King's emblem for his door
Two days left, and
The Thinker
Logically starts to pull away
The Sun King of Swords
Returns
Practical, strategic, realistic
I become Camille
Crazy, irrational, and naive
Wanting to carve the moments
Of passion in marble and bronze
Hoping they would last forever
I become Van Gogh, painting
Scenes of starry nights
From the window of my asylum
Talking to the voices in my head
Ah…the fragile minds
Of those who love too much
Are forever damned
They are better off
In Dali's realms
Where time is melting and worlds
are merging and entering
Madness in the same breath
As someone who sighs
Inhaling night jasmine,
Sipping on cold champagne

While staring at the starry night

…And then dropping dead.

…But through a waking death

A lucid Dali dream
A parallel universe where
Anything can happen
Appears
Everything is desert-like, a
Schizophrenic nightmare of
Fish coming out of a pomegranate
Eating a tiger
A kaleidoscope of chaos with
Elephants on stilts
Reflections not of swans but
Burning giraffes
Or was it elephants?
A world of possibilities
You don't love Dali
You buy a dusty Tolkien Anthology
From a bookstore
Appearing during a time warp
On a lost road
A kiss as we cross every bridge
Unique front doors
Will be the door to our future home
Garden mazes, labyrinths

Sentimental voids and surrealism
Floral fantasies
Montmartre has secret stories
Of our past lifetime
We lived near Sacre Coeur
Notre Dame and the alter to Lost Children
We all know loss
His famous moustache and
Crazy antics
Begging to be seen alive and not the
Dead version of his brother
Born in Spain,
But his soul is still alive in Paris
Breton and the Surrealists
Haunt the gardens
I am Gala, his muse
But I am allergic to bees
Tristan and Isolde's passion and tragedy
Dreamlike daze
Of a perfect desire
But instead
He buys a replica of *The Thinker,*
Sitting on the gates of Hell
And I buy *The Kiss,*
The lovers fated to wander forever through Hell
Drinking makes it work
I open another bottle
I also buy *The Sakountala* to
Create two beautiful bookends

But you will only see me as *The Implorer*
Holding your coat as you close the door
Screaming in many languages
As I look up at you from Hell
And you look down
With your empty eyes
And think for an eternity of all the reasons
We will never work

In a multiverse of endless possibilities…
No animals suffer
No sentient beings suffer
We all love our spirit animal(s)
And you…
… don't have any allergies

James Dean

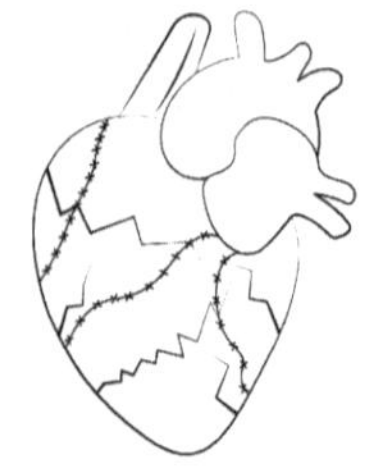

I stalked you
I did
You ghosted me and
I wanted to see
If you were okay
You are surprisingly easy
To find
Damn
That smile
The way those long fingers
Touched me
My warm skin still craves you, but
It is my soul that
Searches desperately
For you
How I wake with thoughts
Of our bodies
Coming together under the stars
Your minty chapstick
Kissing me everywhere
You are

Moving to California
Closer than Ireland
But it feels further
I knew that was a good possibility
Before stalking you
And suddenly,
I am calling you
James Dean
Mr. Dean
Mr. James Byron Dean
And singing
Taylor's song,
"James Dean, daydream…look in your eyes."
On an annoying loop
I try to picture you in a white T-shirt
But that doesn't work
It is your smile and your eyes
I see you flying down the highway
In a silver Spyder
You are twice his age
But you can still "live fast and
leave a good-looking corpse."
The girl next to you, with
Dark glasses and a
Silk scarf tied around her hair
A permanent pout
Beating you down
With disdain
A real bitch

No… that's my jealousy
My shadow side
My parasite
It's not what I want for you
I want you to find love
…Rewind

The girl next to you, with
Dark glasses and a
Silk scarf tied around her hair
She is smiling at you
Her eyes dance
Her hands catch the air
Her long, straight hair
Blows around her face
And you are happy
You love her
Your hand rests on her long leg
And she tells you that she
Dreamt of you last night
You ask what happened
"You were seducing me
In King Louis' court
You were charming
And had many admirers
And you looked so funny
All those ruffles
And high heels
We broke into a forbidden area
And explored the rooms

We were whispering
Of course, we found a bedroom
Huge red velvet pillows
And a red velvet canopy
We stopped and tried it out.
I never thought you would
Get me out of all those laces."
You kiss her hand
Explaining it was a past life
You had seen that, too
She takes your hand and places it under her skirt
And leans back
With the sun and breeze on her face
And your fingers circling
As you speed down the highway
"Her red lip classic smiles"
And unlike James Dean
Your Pier Angeli
Doesn't care about your religion
She cares about you
Will you give up your Marilyns,
Your Ursulas, and
Your men?
When your mother named you
After Lord Byron,
Did she know what she did?
He loved many
He loved hard, but
was also a romantic

At heart
He said,
“There are four questions of value in life…
What is sacred?
Of what is the spirit made?
What is worth living for, and
What is worth dying for?
The answer to each is the same.
Only love.”

Will you let yourself love her?
OR
Are you going to live
In the past?

Will you continue worshipping
A dedicated barbed wire memorial
At a junction of
Bras, sunglasses, and hats
Your speeding Spyder spinning in
Spirals singing songs of
Slinging swords slaying
A HEART that
Smashed into a 1950
Ford Custom Coupe
On the intersection of
Highways 41 and 46
Becoming a pile of mutilated metal
And never...
...Beating again?

In a multiverse of endless possibilities…
We change the world
There are no more refugees
Drowning in our seas
Because there is no more war
Unconditional love is
Everywhere

Visions

The books we read
The movies we watch
Hold truths
For those who are looking
A movie watched
Before you knew
The things you do
Were full of signs
Right in your face
But if you are asleep
You will never see it
And once your eyes
Are open
You can't unsee it
I didn't understand
How thin the veil is
Between the worlds

Until the spiders were
In my bathroom
One white
One black
Creating a web
Above the chair
Where I set
My red velvet robe
I blew gently
On the web
Hoping they would climb up
Instead of down
But with my breath
The bathroom wall
The web
And spiders turned into
A strange light
From a strange world
A Portal to Beyond
I had a second
To decide to enter
But I stepped back instead
And the portal closed
It all disappeared
Including my two new friends
I was standing there
Naked
Frozen
Seconds passed

Regret soon followed
I had had the chance to travel
And I stepped backwards
Instead of forward
I wrap the towel around me
And start blowing gusts of air
My hands are trying to find
The tear
I swore the next time
To be ready
Months later
Still waiting…
But I know
If I hold my arm out straight
Another world is
Within its reach
I thought you would believe me
You know people that
Have lost time
Have entered other
Universes while opening
Their front door
You smile and shake your head
You explain that people
Often see things in their minds
From movies that they imagine
Into real life
I can see your point
But I add—

If I could have created
A moment like this
I promise
It wouldn't have been in
My bathroom and
I would have been dressed
We both laugh
This entire date…
Is full of signs
Somehow, my GPS stopped working
So I was late
My stomach has ached since
I arrived
The pouring rain
Drowned our table of food
I whisper
To my Guardians to
Please leave me alone
To just have this night
They are insistent in
Telling me to let go
I try to tell them NO
I argue with them in my head
You ask me why I am so quiet
And I think I must have had
Tears forming
As I grab your hand
And you tell me that
My daughter had told you

I think you are cute
So funny…
….surely you know that!
I decide to grasp this moment
Take photographs in my mind
How I wish we were aligned
Our feet are stepping
In two different worlds
And I know this is the last time
The kids spill their beer
On the table across from us
You watch them longingly
Maybe wishing to be young
And I look longingly into
What I had wished for us
My heart fills with
Unconditional love
And with this thought came
A sense of peace
And relief
And then I think
I can pretend that
Maybe you aren't even
Really here
You are just a vision
That you don't deem real
You are my
Beautiful, strange light
That is shining too bright

And tragically
…will only disappear.

Shadows and Seers

It is, as you say
A shadow that sneaks up behind you
You know it's there
You might run
But it is patient
It knows you will
Eventually
Grow tired…
It is different for everyone
When he grabs me
And I spiral

I see the young Syrian boy
In the red shirt
Lying face down in the sea
His body rocks with the gentle waves
A permanent sleep
In a desperate attempt
To reach Europe

Not that Greece would have been
Beautiful
Living in mud
In a tent
With little food
And disease
But you would not be face down
Rocking in the sea
Wearing red
I wish I could have saved you
I post your picture on FB
And people yell
They do not want to see
Such a disturbing image
They want to look at food
And airbrushed smiles
I lose faith
I sit on the shore
Holding your small hand
Night after night
I whisper to you
The boy in red
While the surf rocks you gently

It is as the The Jedi Master gasped,
"I felt a great disturbance in the Force
as if millions of voices suddenly cried out
in terror and were suddenly silenced."
And he couldn't save them.

The jumping man jumps
Over and over
I feel ill
As I fall
As I make the decision
To fall
Over being burned alive
The photo shows
The hanged man
Resigned to fate
I worry that he is conscious
As he falls
Such a long way down
What are the thoughts
Going through his mind
There is no hope
We are all the jumping man
Falling down the rabbit hole
The towers fall
The ash covers the streets
The survivors breathe in the ash of the dead
As they circle in confusion
Planes still explode
And crash
People continue to die
For years
And I cannot save them

The voices cry out in terror
A great disturbance in the force

Alone in the house
The baby cries
In the empty crib
The mobile of stars spins
On the ceiling
As a music box plays
My hair fans the teal marble
My hands run over the empty womb
You cry and cry
But I cannot reach you
He took you
The one in grey
Your name was on the list
To never breathe in
The polluted air
The half-finished nursery
Of blue and yellow
Will never hold you
And I wish I could die
To be together
Instead of this useless
Vessel
Left here with a blade and bathtub
Tissues and a small coffin
With clothes that are not my own
I awaken from

The fog
And cut them up
I have always hated yellow flowers
The teal marble
Becomes a sea
And I stay there for hours
Listening to you
In my mind
The invisible rocking chair rocks
In the corner
He comes home to find me
Asleep on the floor
In the dark
Only the stars circling on the ceiling
Yelling for his food
Yelling for his wife
Both are nonexistent
He says that he does not know me
That I am mad
That I am useless
He grabs the mobile
From your crib and
Smashes it
I will never forgive him
For this
I am surprised that he
Can still see me
Because I am already dead
The front door slams

And I barely breathe
Alone
Amongst the cut-up clothes,
Broken plastic, batteries, and
Music still desperately
Trying to turn the stars
And the invisible rocking chair rocks
And you cry from a great distance
And I cannot save you

This is what it is like
For me
For you
It will be different
But the shadow
Laughs as he climbs on
Your back
And he becomes heavier and heavier
Running becomes laboured steps
Drowning from the weight
Of all the pain
And cries from around the world
The Universe
The headlines
The news
The eyes and energy
Of everyone
Scream out in pain
And I cannot save them
They are never going home

Images come fast
Head aches
Hollow brown eyes stare out of skeletons
Starving
Or bleeding
And we complain that we have nothing
The Italian boat watches them drown
They are not welcome
The priests hold their heads in shame
As molested, young boys cry forever
And girls are sold
To disgusting old men
Emaciated polar bears
Float on icebergs
His father puts his hands down my shirt
He laughs as he grabs my ass
And corners me
In my own house
The orangutan holds onto
The falling tree in vain
And their bodies are covered with the ash
Of the dead
Which floats in the streets
His body rocks in the gentle surf
The falling man falls
Incessant heat
Dead chickens everywhere
A bonfire of books and photographs
Lit by the rage of love

Bombs go off
Limbs scatter
A funeral procession
Marches in my mind
Thousands of people die
While millions quarantine
A dog waits in the driveway
For me
But I am never going home
The cats bleed and die on repeat
The chanting stops
The drums are still
The stars stop spinning
Moving hurts
So, I stay on the teal marble floor
For what feels like forever
I hold his tiny hand
As his body rocks in the surf
And the baby cries
From far away
While the rocking chair rocks
And the cicadas scream
And the fire consumes
The memories
As the world dies and
The shadow follows me
Across the Earth
I cannot run fast enough
And she waits,

Looking up the driveway
For me
Next to
The dead cats’ graves
But I cannot save them
And I am never going home.

Silence

How are we connected?
I ask the sky
My Guardians
The Tarot
The swinging pendulum
Besides that thin red thread
That forms in bed
Why does he consume me?
Why is it so intense?
It doesn't make sense…
Suddenly, a random FB group
Freezes
On my feed
And I click to see the members
1,978 souls
I decided to look at them all
Skimming,
Scanning,

Stopping
There you are
With your daughter
I feel frozen and faint
Confused and crazy
…And you joined a year and two months
Before I did
All this time
We were in
Similar circles and
You pretended to be surprised
And ignorant of
Sigils, spells and libations
This explains it
A magical incantation was woven
With my wonder and ramblings
Your shock, shy, surprise
A religious ruse
Sometimes, spells said in
Silence
Hold more power

In a multiverse of endless possibilities…

Waning Crescent Moon

There is a Bench

There is a bench
On a beach
Staring out at an ocean
It belongs to a large house
That never has any lights on
A widow's watch on the roof
At least five bedrooms
No one sleeps there
This will be our home
I claim it
I declare it
Squatters rights
My manifestation
Law of attraction
I say it is so
And so it is
You laugh
I smile

Let’s go in for one night
You tell me I am crazy
We will lose our jobs
We will go to jail
We don’t know how to jimmy a lock
All valid points
Although it won’t be our
First break-in
You smile
And explain an open-door
Is an invitation
There are no tools involved
So we plan some
Stakeouts
We meet at the bench
On several evenings
We sit there for hours
We eat dinner
Write poems
Read to each other
Take walks
Argue
Create sand art
Watch the stars
Discuss the universe
Argue
Drink red wine
Laugh
Kiss

Make love
We make a pact
Every July 20th
From now until death
We will meet here
It must have been
Nice for the bench
To not be alone and
Somewhere in all that
Fun
We forgot our plan
To sleep in the house
We forgot our plan
To change the world
I fall in love with the bench
It still sits here
Looking out at an ocean
I still visit
But I sit alone
I remember your dinners
On paper plates
The plastic silverware breaking
Using our hands
I remember my magick
That you never loved
I remember embracing every excuse
To be next to you
Now it is just me,
The bench, and

The empty house
What a waste
We could have filled it with love
Like the memories of this bench
I engrave the year on it
And a big “D”
We could have had 1920s parties
I can hear the music
See the flappers
We could have invited poets
We could have invited painters
Champagne flowing
Fingers flying across the keys
Of the grand piano
The saxophone swaying
Beautiful red lipstick
Singing
We smile at one another
From across the room
I point up
And we race to the roof
We pace the widow's wharf
Looking out at the ocean
Looking for a ship
With no clothes on
This never happens
In this lifetime
Maybe it was our past life
We placed this bench here

We sat here until we died
And we met here again
We will find photos of us
Inside the dark house
I will find my hidden jewels
And old journals
You shake your head
Smiling,
Gazing down the beach
Mystery and magic
Following new footprints
Pacts are forgotten
Dreams die
The music never plays
The lights never come on
The rooms are never slept in
There is never laughter
Nor is there love
The big beautiful windows remain dark
And I am still reading on
An empty bench
Looking out on a vast ocean
My only companion is
The widow's ghost
Which could also be me
Staring from the roof
Of the empty house
Always wondering when
You are coming home

In a multiverse of endless possibilities…
You call that Friday
I contact you on your birthday
We meet at the bench
You take 17 seconds to text
We remain friends

In a multiverse of endless possibilities
We must be happy somewhere…

The Games We Must Play

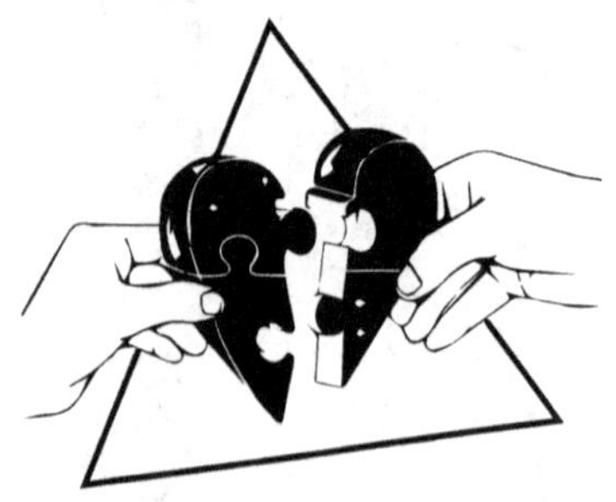

At least Christian Grey
Was clear
About his intentions
A nondisclosure
Was given
A contract was drawn up
Negotiations at the table
A bright red playroom
A lifetime of trauma
Wrapped up in a
Handsome package
Full of kinky escapes
And expensive bows
You play games
That blur
Nice guy and Player
Which is the true definition
Of a good player
How do you draw your

Gameboard
Strategize your week
"Which day would you like to meet?
Friday or Saturday?"
If I say Friday,
Who is your Saturday?
I don't ask
I am a strong,
Independent woman
This is the game we must play
I try
I pretend it doesn't matter
Because in the end
You will see
What I know
I know you
I have known you
Through time
It is so apparent to me
But to you
I am just another piece
Of a children's puzzle
A minor mystery to be solved
I am only as fascinating
As my secrets
And I tell you all
I move down in rotation
When I am switched to
Monday or Tuesday

And then once a month
Until the breadcrumbs
Are barely visible
And I sit lost
In the forest
Of lies
Not directly told
But I listen to
What you
Don't say
...And you don't say a lot
I don't know how
You do it
How
Each one feels
Seen
Only to slowly
Zoom out
And Fade
I knew this was the game
Every therapist raves,
"Catch and Release"
"Catch and Release"
...Now I need therapy
And I could see it all
And I played along
You have that charm
That James Dean
Twinkle in your eyes

That way to make me
Trust you
Feel like I am different
I am exactly what
You have been looking for
I am your Anastasia Steele
You see us in that big house
We are having parties
We make love
Tied to the railing of
The widow perch
When the time is right
You will buy this house
And my heart soars
Every day for the rest of my life
I might wake up next to you
That's the game
The make-believe
I wish I could
Laugh and play along
Dress the part
Enjoy the now
Pretend, pretend, pretend
But my stupid heart
Is not strong
I love you
I tried not to
Your voice
Your touch

Your kiss
Your thoughts
I miss them, and they—
They are with someone else
Who has to wonder
Who is Saturday
But one day
You will meet your match
The tables will turn
And you will become
Monday
Guard your heart
My Love
The three of swords
Has already
Made you what you are

I sound bitter
And I am not
I am grateful
You saw me
You encouraged me
You were my
Catalyst of change
You convinced me
That I could change the world
You told me to be
Whomever
I want to be

I quit my job
I travel
Money poor
But life rich
It is a life without you
Radio silence
Your last words were,
I will call you on Friday
Ha!…at least I ended as a Friday
And I think it is more of a
Blessing than a curse
Because you are a mixture
Of pain and love…
Some Fridays
A small tear
Threatens to fall and
I smile at the
Thought of a call
That will never happen.

In a multiverse of endless possibilities…
We are on the timeline where
I don’t miss you
Every night
As I am
Closing my eyes
And reaching for your ghost

A City I Used to Love

The idea was to publish
Poems about you
Maybe a book or two
And then wrap them up
In silver, or red and green
Shiny paper
And a huge bow
Send them in a bigger box
In hopes that the bow
Would survive the
Christmas rush
To a general address
Found online
With your title,
To: Mr. Dean
You would smile
And think,
"I forgot about her
I should invite her to dinner."
And we would meet

In Boston
Because we love Boston
And it is a beautiful restaurant
Candles and soft holiday music
The scent of cinnamon
And twinkly lights
I am dressed in a green dress
I have lost tons of weight
And my auburn hair flows to my waist
(Hey, it is my masochistic manifestation
Taking place on another timeline…
I might as well be thin.)
We share a bottle of wine
And I already know
That walking will be tricky
Your smile
Your eyes
The way you hold my hand
As you passionately
Explain the chaos
That is this world
I tell you about the hot mess
That is the refugee crisis
Here and abroad
I try your saffron rice
You finish my lemon-pepper asparagus
It is a natural exchange
It always has been
We watch the violinist

And sigh
I would brush my hand on your cheek
And you would awkwardly continue
With your personal news
You have moved
Across the country
Which I already knew
But then you explain
That you are in love
With a witch who has
Spellbound you
You smile
That smile
And my heart beats
Irregularly
I smile and say something
Positive and grand
But in my mind,
There are sirens,
Emergency alerts,
A voice that sounds
Like my own is yelling,
Sit up straight
No crying
Look him in the eyes
And tell him that you are
Happy for him
I am happy for him
"I am happy for you," I say

You say that finally
You are feeling love
And we clink our glasses
Together and laugh
The bubbles go down easily
Past the heart that is
Crying,
"Mayday, mayday, mayday!"
As the three of swords
All twist deeper
And the body is shaking on
The verge of imploding
My soul goes into shock
And I sit here smiling
Trying not to look like a
Deranged mannequin
Sharing a slice of cheesecake
Drinking the last sip
Of celebratory bubbles
We sparkle, and I think
I deserve an Oscar
I don't think you can tell
That every fantasy
Every dream
Every poem
Was a wish
Sent to star systems
That obviously
No longer exist

And I wrap my scarf
Tightly around my neck
You help me put on my coat
You tell me that
You love the way I smell
Like jasmine and rain
We hug
Like long-lost friends
Promise to keep in touch
I turn to leave
Quickly because
It is the final countdown
To complete meltdown
You yell, "Are you sure you are okay?"
"Yes, of course!
My brother lives just up here!"
And we wave
And I think
This is the last time
I will ever see you
I am running now
On ice, in heels
Thank god it is so cold
That the tears are
Freezing
The free-flowing faucet
Turning
My eyelashes into
Tiny icicles

As I wander aimlessly on
Streets I don't know
Searching for a
Brownstone apartment
Amongst all the
Brownstone apartments
In a city, I used to love…

In a multiverse of endless possibilities…
We have no regrets
And your guitar
No longer "Gently Weeps"

The Last Christmas

Another Christmas night passes
Another promise to move on
To bring in the New Year
Differently
Candles reflected in the windows
As the tree lights twinkle at the stars
The waning crescent moon
Shines
On the war of religions
The war of land
The war of greed
Genocide
Missiles flash like
Far away comets
Foretelling fatalities
There might never be another
Night like this one
And yet, I still do not move on
Why should I?

If I want to love you
Feel you
For the ever of my life
Whether that be moments or months
It is mine
On this possible last Christmas
Nothing is entrapping your energy
Except for that thin red thread
I feel you alive
But you could be dead
You were never here
On Christmas
You never sat in front of the fire
Kissing my neck
Clinking our champagne
Eyes meeting
Clothes sliding off
While the children slept
You never hung the ornaments on
Traditional trees
Or tied the
The presents with bright bows
Only to be ripped open
With wide smiles
The whole world has lost
Its childish wonder
The last cries of the birth of a new life
Sounds through the empty halls
A new species

Will never walk
Extinction has ended the evolution
And all the voices singing
To a god
That can no longer
Hear them over the bombs
Sees them in pieces,
Masterpieces splattered
The last Christmas song,
"I'll be home for Christmas."
Plays on repeat for eternity
And the Roomba keeps groaning
Circling and cleaning
But it can only smear the blood and
Move the ashes
There are no homes left
Only empty shells
The few people left alive, the
Wanderers are wailing, walking,
Wondering when the wind will
Whip them away, and the
Stockings will always hang empty
Nailed on broken chimneys
As the houses crumble and
Our bones blow in the hot wind
Our hair joins the tumbleweeds
Trees attached to stands with glitter
Blow by
A reminder of what was

The poisonous oceans churn
The sun turns its back
As fire fills the sky
And the moon
Searches desperately
For signs of life
No memory
Of love
Anywhere
And still… I will love you.

In a multiverse of endless possibilities…
Scott Hutchison isn't
"Floating in the Forth" in a
"Death Dream" and
We all write music together

Our Story in Haiku

The sand in your teeth
Moon and stars glowing on water
I felt our past lives

My almond eyes close
Quantum jumping through space-time
Your grey eyes open

Your smile shines through words
"I will call you on Friday."
I wait forever

That day in July
When humans walked on the moon
I won't forget you

You hate Prosecco
I love the taste of your lips
We make a new wine

You smell beautiful
Like jasmine from long ago
I remember you

I remember you
Giving me an amulet
In King Louis' court

We needed more help
To protect our broken hearts
In the past… and now

I am not afraid
I will love you forever
You forgot my name

Unconditional
Love expands throughout the world
Love is everywhere.

Writing You Out Of My Heart

Today is July 20th and
I didn't go to
Our bench
Of course, you broke
The pact long ago
I, however, feel like
I need to apologize to
The bench
Ridiculous, I know
You once asked me to
Write you a poem
That only you would know
Was about you
You probably don't even
Remember saying this
"You're so vain," kept flashing
But now
I think it was a goodbye

I wrote all of these
Some true-ish
Some completely fictional
But all describing feelings
And thoughts
Surrounding you…
Some came out okay
Others were a stretch
Some are terrible
A 21-day challenge
All poems
To get over you
Therapy-wise
The cheapest way
To write you out of
My heart
The thin red thread
Still remains
But
Unconditional love
Has already accepted
That I can love you
And be so happy for you
And let you go
Be love
Be healthy
Be happy
I hope to see
Your smile again

One day…
In this life or the next
For now…
In the words of my favourite poet:
(Changing “her/she” to “you”)

“Because through nights like this one, I held (you) in my arms
my soul is not satisfied that it has lost (you).
Though this be the last pain that (you) make me suffer
and these the last verses that I write for (you).”

Pablo Neruda
Tonight I Can Write (The Saddest Lines)

Goodbye, My Love… At least… on this timeline.

In a multiverse of endless possibilities…
You. Love. Me.

17 Seconds

I timed myself typing phrases today:

Sorry, I can't talk today.	8.43 seconds
	+
Happy New Year!	4.60 seconds
	+
How are you?	3.61 seconds
	= 16.64 seconds

Rounding up = 17 seconds

17 seconds doesn't seem like it is expecting too much!
…And I type pretty slowly.

How quickly and easily those words could have made me smile…
…and kept us as friends.

What a waste…

In a multiverse of endless possibilities…

Fever Dream

Waking and searching for
The can of mangos
In the wrong cupboards
In the wrong country
Where am I?
He jumps
Does he think as he falls,
"Would fire have been better?"
I have always loved you
And the rocking chair rocks
For a thousand years
In past lives and
Parallel universes
We kiss
I smell of jasmine and rain
Mango juice down your neck
Sand in your teeth
Who are you?
She stares up the driveway
For me
But I am never going home
Time melts in the desert

I cannot save them
The Hall of Mirrors and Light
Knowing
Destiny
A religious ruse
The stars keep turning
You cry from a great distance
Refugees fleeing for their lives
Walking miles upon miles
Orion's belt
The stars align
Starseeds
Cats bleeding from their eyes
The three of swords twist deeper
They trusted me
He betrayed them
Dancing on the beach
And glow up into heaven
The stars answer back
With the hope of a better life
A promise
A dream
Death
A bonfire of rage and love
A henna map
To the universe
Paris
Giza
There is a bench

The windows remain dark
Teasing me with a feather
Your smile
Missing you
Van Gogh loved too much
Why didn't I listen to the signs?
Why did you say I could trust you?
It's okay
Someday, I am going to be with you
In this life or the next
I stepped backward
Instead of forward
This warm skin stuck to mine
Do I still wander?
The night lights dance
A kaleidoscope of colours
Unconditional love
Pulling away
Twin flames
Karmics
Making sand angels
In a city I used to love
Worshipping each other
Let me whisper in your ear
Past lives and light languages
You will only see me as *The Implorer*
Lying face down in the sea
His body rocks with the gentle waves
And I cannot save him

A catalyst for change
And you look down
With your empty eyes
And think for an eternity of all the reasons
We will never work
Imprinting
An idea of a better world
Stars falling
His Gatsbian hand
Reaching for Ireland
James Dean
Cruising in California
Diving into your mind
Makes me want your skin
These are your stars
21 days and a book of poems
Writing you out of my heart
Versailles and Paris
Dali, Monet, Rodin, and Camille
We thought we could
Change the world
Leaving the sand in my hair
The hot nights
No air conditioners
Sleeping in tents
I will never find enough water
Disease runs through the camps
The fever eats our brains
My sanity screams, clawing

I don't recognize the
Sobs, shrieks, and howls
Emanating from my soul
I can see the stars through
A hole in the top
You are seeing the same moon
You awaken as
I fall asleep
I want to taste your air
Smell the rain
Feel the mango
As it drips down
Your tongue
Creating symbols
Across my body
The Great Pyramids
And extraterrestrials
Alice Paul starved
For what she believed
Silence is so final
The games we play
We make a new wine
Making wishes on stars
Mon Chérie
You never think of me
The veil is so thin
Divine Runner, run
No memory of love
Anywhere

They shoved tubes down her throat
The fight will never end
And still…I will love you
We are one
We all meet
Under The Tree of Life
To watch it burn
Our hearts smoulder
While we hold hands
On “Solsbury Hill”
And chant
Wishing we could save
Christmas, with
Missiles lighting up the night sky
I really thought we could save us
Death
War
Genocide
And the moon searches desperately
For signs of life
You are never coming home
Wandering alone
Weeping
Looking for a fucking can of mangos
As I disintegrate into dust

...Thank you for reading.